RAT

Deborah Chancellor

FRANKLIN WATTS
LONDON•SYDNEY

First published in 2007 by Franklin Watts
338 Euston Road, London NW1 3BH

Franklin Watts Australia
Level 17/207 Kent Street
Sydney NSW 2000

Editor: Rachel Tonkin and Julia Bird
Designer: Proof Books
Picture researcher: Diana Morris

Picture credits:
A1Pix: 4; Arco Images/Alamy: 5, 6, 13, 25;
Krys Bailey/Marmotta-PhotoArt: 17; Vladimir Georgievsky: 22;
Elena Kenunen: 9; Jean Michel Labat/Ardea: 26;
PetStockBoys: front cover, 1, 29; Steiner/Arco Images/Alamy: 12, 21.

All other photography: Andy Crawford

Every attempt has been made to clear copyright.
Should there be any inadvertent omission please
apply to the publisher for rectification.

With thanks to Jan Bell and Lucy Milne, and Lucy's pet rats, Nipper
and Rafferty.

A CIP catalogue record for this book
is available from the British Library

ISBN: 978 0 7496 7061 0

Dewey Classification: 636.9'352

Printed in China

Franklin Watts is a division of Hachette Children's Books.

Contents

What is a rat?

Rats have been bred and kept as pets for many years and make fantastic family pets. Anyone who has ever kept pet rats will tell you so. But sadly, some people confuse domestic rats with wild rats, and do not like the idea of rats as pets. This is a mistake, because wild rats are very different from domestic ones.

Pet rats

Pet rats are the same species as the wild brown rat, but this is where the similarity ends. They are much less aggressive than wild rats, and bond very well with their human owners. They are bred for their pretty looks and friendly temperament.

Bucks

Male rats are called bucks. They are larger and lazier than female rats, with a coarser coat and a musky smell. Bucks like to mark out their territory with a few drops of their urine. This habit is known as 'scent-marking'.

Does

Female rats are called does. They are smaller and more active than males. They have a softer coat and don't smell musky like male rats. About once every five days, a female rat is 'on heat' for about 12 hours. This is when she is looking for a male partner. During this time she is more jumpy and active than normal.

Wild rats are often found on rubbish dumps or in sewers. These unwelcome pests can spread disease.

Baby rats are born blind and rely on their mother to feed them for the first four weeks of their life.

In the family

Rats are rodents. The rodent family includes many other small furry pets, such as hamsters, gerbils and mice.

Having kittens

A female rat is pregnant for 21-24 days before having a litter of between 2 and 20 babies. The tiny babies are called kittens, and they are born bald and blind. They need to drink their mother's milk for at least four weeks.

Blind as a rat

Rats first open their eyes when they are two weeks old, and they do not have great eyesight. However, their sense of hearing and smell is very sharp – much better than a human's.

Questions & Answers

* **Is it better to have male or female pet rats?**
Rats should be kept in same sex pairs or groups. It is up to you to choose whether you want to keep males or females – they behave slightly differently, but both are just as good to keep as pets.

* **Can you smell a rat's scent-markings?**
No, because a male rat only uses a few small drops of urine to mark out his territory. Humans can't smell this, but other rats can.

* **Can I keep a wild rat as a pet?**
No, it is against the law to keep wild rats as pets as they are classed as vermin.

Do you really want rats?

Rats make excellent pets because they have lots of character and personality, and are very friendly. They are not particularly expensive to buy or feed. But it is quite hard work looking after rats for the whole of their lives. Before you buy pet rats, you must be sure you can give them the time and care they need.

Playmates

Just like dogs, rats can be affectionate to their owners. If you are kind and attentive to your pet rats, they will bond with you and will be lots of fun to play with. They will easily repay all the attention and affection you are prepared to give them. But your pets will quickly become unhappy if you don't take the time to play with them every day.

Free time

Rats need time to roam outside their cages every day, or they soon will become bored and unhappy. Before you decide to get pet rats, you must check with your family that you will be allowed to let your rats do this.

If you spend time playing with your rats, you will enjoy each other's company.

Be prepared!

If you have pet rats, you can't have a day off just because you feel like it. You must be prepared to clean their cage regularly, give them food and water every day, and spend time each day playing with them. If you don't think you will be able to do this, then you had better not keep pet rats.

Celebrity rat

Beatrix Potter, the famous children's author and illustrator, had a white pet rat called Sammy.

Living space

Rats need to live indoors, as they can get too hot or cold outside. This means that you must have enough space and a suitable place to put a big rat cage in your home.

Do your homework

It is important to find out a lot about rats before you decide to get a pair or small group of them. Read a few books and look at some good websites (see page 31). If you can, talk to people you know who keep rats. You and your family must know what you are taking on before you buy your new pets.

Questions & Answers

How long do I need to play with my rats every day?
Most rats need about an hour's play outside their cages each day.

Can rats learn tricks?
Yes, rats are clever enough to learn simple tricks. For example, you can teach a rat to run the quickest way through a maze. Build the maze up with books or bricks, and place a tasty treat at the other end of the maze for your rat to find.

Will my pet rats recognise me?
Yes, and they will quickly learn to enjoy being with you. When they see you coming, they will run to the front of their cage to meet you.

Do your research with someone in your family, so you can learn about rats together.

7

Choosing your rats

Before you go out to buy your pet rats, you must get their cage ready for them. Make sure you have all the food, bedding and accessories that they will need when they come home with you (see pages 18 and 19). Go to a good rat breeder or a high-quality pet shop to choose your rats. If the rats for sale have been well cared for, they will be healthy and sociable.

Breeders are best

It is best to buy rats from a rat breeder. This is because the baby rats won't have had the stress of moving from their birthplace to a pet shop. Also, a rat breeder can show you your chosen rats' parents and siblings. If the whole rat family is healthy, your chosen rats probably will be as well.

Which ones?

Choose a pair of rats that are curious about you, and do not seem nervous when you approach their cage. Baby rats should be handled from a very young age, and should be used to human contact by the time they are bought. As a general rule, never buy a rat if it looks unwell, or if any of its family looks sick.

Try to choose active and friendly rats. They will soon get used to you.

Leaving the nest

Baby rats must stay with their mother for the first four to five weeks of their life. Rats that are taken away from their mother sooner than this can become unhappy and sickly. Your rats should be over six weeks old when you take them home. The person who sells you your rats should be able to say exactly how old they are.

Fancy rats are named after the colour of their fur. A 'Chocolate' fancy rat (left) is a soft brown colour.

Fancy that!

Pet rats are called 'fancy rats', and a group of rats is called a 'mischief'.

Young mother?

If you want to get a pair of female rats, make sure that they were separated from their brothers at five weeks old. This is the age that rats can become parents! If your pair stayed with the whole litter for more than five weeks, one or both of them could be pregnant when you buy them.

Give a rat a home

Some people don't think carefully before they buy rats, and decide they don't want to keep them after a while. The UK National Fancy Rat Society can give you details of how to 'adopt' a homeless rat. It is better to do this if you have kept rats before and are already confident about looking after them.

Questions & Answers

✳ **What colours are rats?**
Rats come in lots of different colours, such as pink-eyed white, black-eyed cream, cinnamon and chocolate.

✳ **Can I buy a rat by myself?**
No, you will need to take an adult with you to buy a rat. Responsible rat breeders and pet shops will not sell to a child under the age of 16 as it is against the law.

✳ **What is the best age to buy?**
It is best to buy a baby rat that is around six weeks old. Older rats take longer to get used to you, and younger ones are too young to leave their mothers.

Handling your rats

When you bring your new rats home, give them as much attention as you can and handle them as often as possible. The more you hold and cuddle your rats, the more fun you will have with them. Don't forget to wash your hands with soap and water after playing with your pets.

Take your time

When you first put your rats in their new cage, give them some time to get used to their new surroundings. Don't pick them up straight away. Put one of your old, unwashed T-shirts in their nest box (see page 19) so that they can get used to your smell. Talk to your pets to let them get used to the sound of your voice.

Holding rats

To pick up your rat, put one hand on its back and scoop up its bottom and back legs with your other hand. Hold your pet against your body for comfort and warmth. Never pick up your rat by its tail or squeeze its body – this will really hurt it.

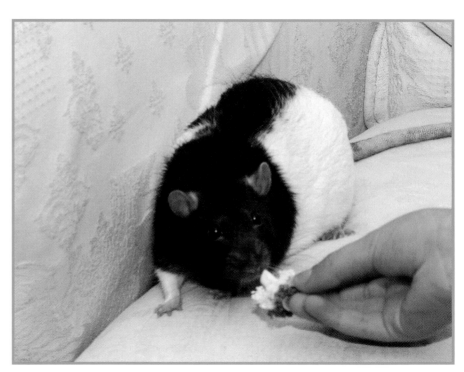

Let your rat get used to you before you give it food from your hand, and try not to feed it titbits too often as it may put on weight.

The first time

Your rat may be a little nervous the first time you pick it up, and may start to wriggle. Hold it calmly and firmly, and don't make any sudden movements as this will frighten your pet. Don't give up if things aren't easy to begin with. Remember that the more you handle your pet rat, the quicker it will become really tame.

Friendly rats

It is important to handle rats when they are very young. If rats are handled a lot when they are tiny, they will bond quickly with their owners.

Good friends

You can never give your rats too much attention. Once you start handling your rats, they will soon get used to you and enjoy being with you. They may well play with your hair, and even lick your face!

Will it bite?

Don't worry that your rat will bite you. Biting is very unusual, and only happens if a rat has been taken by surprise, or is very frightened and defensive. Some 'teenage' male rats or pregnant and nursing females will bite if provoked. If a rat keeps on biting, you may have to take it to a vet to be neutered. Most aggression is hormonal, and can be treated in this way.

Rats like riding on your shoulder or under your jumper.

Questions & Answers

* **Why can't I pick up my rats as soon as I get them home?**
Your rats need to get over the shock of moving away from their first home and get used to their new environment. Leave them for a couple of hours before you pick them up.

* **How do I know when my rats are ready to be held?**
Once your rats have learned to recognise your voice and smell, they will be happy to let you pick them up. They should be confident enough to take food from your hand when you offer it.

* **How long should I spend holding my rats every day?**
There is no set amount of time, but the more the better!

Rat companions

Rats are extremely sociable animals. They like the company of other rats, and enjoy life more if they are kept together in pairs or a small group. Keeping two rats is just as easy as keeping one, and the pair will be much happier and more interesting for you to watch.

These two brothers have been together since birth, and are great friends.

Family group

It is best to keep rats in groups of two or more of the same sex, preferably brothers or sisters from the same litter. They will already know each other well and will be used to one another's company.

Breeding rats

Female rats can have babies when they are just four weeks old, and males can father babies at five weeks old. But it's not advisable for rats to breed so young. If you are serious about breeding from your rats, wait till they are older (about six months), and ask a proper rat breeder for advice.

Old friends

Try to introduce rats to each other before they are ten weeks old. Older rats take longer to get used to new companions. To introduce two older rats, clean out their cages to get rid of territorial scent. Then, dab both rats with scent (such as vanilla essence) and let them play together on neutral ground. After a week, you can put them in the same cage. If they fight a lot, you may have to give up – not all rats get on together.

Out at night

A rat's most active time is in the middle of the night. You will be asleep, so your rat needs the company of other rats at this time!

Play time

Rats are fun to watch as they play. Sometimes, young 'teenage' bucks (four to six months old) may have a fight, but only to work out who is the boss – this isn't usually a serious fight. Does hardly ever fight with each other.

Time out

If two rats are having a fight, never put your hand in their cage to separate them. They may bite you by accident, or in self-defence. Instead, spray both animals with water, or throw a light towel over them. When they have stopped fighting, separate them so they can calm down. Then put them back together in their cage.

Rats are very clean animals, and spend a lot of time grooming each other.

Questions & Answers

✴ **Will two rats bond with each other and become less tame with me?**
No, a pair of rats is much more content and confident than a single rat, and as a result the pair will be very easy to tame.

✴ **How big a cage will a pair of rats need if I keep them together?**
You should allow a minimum of 60 sq cm (two square feet) per rat.

✴ **What if my rats have babies?**
They won't if you have been told the correct sex of your rats, and you keep males and females apart. But if one of your female rats was pregnant when you bought her, she will have babies. If this happens, contact your pet shop or rat breeder for advice.

Housing rats

Your pet rats should live indoors in your home, but if this is not possible, they could also live in your garden shed or garage. They need to be kept inside so they don't get too hot or cold, and are not exposed to wild animals or disease.

Behind bars

Cages with metal bars are best for rats. They allow fresh air to circulate in the cage, and your rats will enjoy experiencing the sounds and smells that come their way. A wire cage also provides an excellent climbing frame for your playful pets. You can stroke your rats through the bars, and feed them treats every now and then.

Rats need lots of room, and will make good use of all the space you give them.

Choosing a cage

Get a tall and roomy wire cage, with a plastic or metal tray underneath that is easy to clean. The bars should be close together, so your rats can't escape. For the same reason, make sure that all the panels and doors are secure. A wooden hutch is not a good idea as your rats will chew the wood, and plastic tanks are not recommended because their ventilation is poor.

Bigger is better

The bigger the cage the better it is – rats can't have too much room to play. Each of your rats needs at least 60 square centimetres of living space. Check the exact size of a cage before you buy it, because every square centimetre makes a difference to a rat. Make sure you have enough room at home for your cage before you buy it.

Hot and cold

The ideal temperature for a rat is between 7°C and 24°C. Your rats may become ill if they are colder or hotter than this.

Too hot or cold?

Rats don't like to be too hot or too cold, but they usually find it harder to cope with very high temperatures. If it gets hotter than 30°C rats can die from heat stroke. Make sure your rats' cage is out of direct sunlight and away from radiators. Remember that your rats don't like cold either, so keep their cage away from draughts. If it gets very cold, give them extra warm bedding.

Questions & Answers

* **Is it OK to buy a second-hand rat cage?**
Yes, but make sure you disinfect, rinse and dry it thoroughly before you put your new rats in it.

* **Can I keep my rats in a hamster cage?**
No, not even three-storey hamster cages are big enough for rats, and they don't give your rats enough chances to climb.

* **Isn't a wire cage too draughty for my rats?**
No, they need the ventilation, but they will also need a warm, sheltered nest box (see page 19) to sleep in.

Prime position

Think carefully about where to put your rats' cage. If you can, place it up high on a table or chest of drawers in a busy part of your home, such as the living room. This will make it easy for you and your family to see your rats and interact with them. Rats are sociable creatures, so they will also enjoy being able to see you and your family.

Keep your rats somewhere in your home where they can become part of the family. Always make sure the cage is securely closed.

Roaming rats

Rats are intelligent animals, so they soon get bored with their cage and need to go exploring. Let your rats roam free outside their cage every day. You will need to make a few small changes to the room you let them loose in, but it is well worth the trouble you take to give your rats this exciting experience.

Rat room

Choose a room in your home that your rats can roam around in safely. Ask an adult to help you 'rat-proof' the room. You will have to remove or cover anything that could be a danger to your pets. You may also need to protect your furniture. Male rats scent-mark their territory with drops of urine, so you may decide to cover some furniture.

Electric danger

All rats like to chew, so you must ask an adult to move all electrical cables out of your pets' reach. If one of your rats chews through a wire, it could die from an electric shock. If it isn't possible to move all the cables out of the way, cover them with hosepipe or aquarium tubing.

Don't let a roaming rat get under blankets or inside furniture, or someone might sit on it by accident!

Getting ready

When you 'rat-proof' a room, move all your precious items out of the way, for example clothes, books and fragile ornaments. Remove all houseplants as well, because some plants are poisonous to rats. Your rats could also make a big mess by digging into the plant pots!

Rats will take a fancy to any small objects that they can carry off to chew.

Rat's-eye view

It may help to lie on the floor and look around, imagining that you are as small as a rat. Can you see any rat-sized holes, or good hiding places? You will need to 'rat-proof' these. Ask an adult to seal any cracks in the skirting or floorboards. Finally, close all the doors and windows to the room, so that there are no escape routes.

Stay indoors

Only let your rats loose in a room that has been specially prepared for this purpose. Never be tempted to let your rats roam free outside the house. If they got lost, they would quickly starve or be killed by wild animals.

Roaming time

Rats need to roam free for at least an hour every day.

Questions & Answers

* **Can I leave the room when my rats are roaming free?**
  Rats can easily get into trouble, so it's best not to leave them on their own. If you do need to leave the room your rats are in for an urgent reason, ask someone in the family to 'mind' them while you are gone.

* **Should I take my shoes off when my rats are roaming?**
  Yes, because you may tread on them by accident and hurt your pets.

* **Can my rats play with my other pets?**
  Don't let your rats loose near a cat or dog, as either of these animals could kill your rats if they wanted to. Take great care introducing your pets to each other, and never leave them alone together. You must also be aware that rats are predators, so don't let them get close to any other small animals or birds.

Litter and bedding

Rats like to have a nice, cosy place to sleep. You must put clean, soft bedding in your rats' nest box, so they have a warm, secure bed to rest in. Your rats enjoy eating and drinking, but this means they will wet and soil their cage. You will need to put special litter at the bottom of their cage to soak up the mess and stop it from smelling.

Rat litter

Buy the right kind of litter to line the bottom of your rats' cage. It is best to use shredded cardboard or paper-based litters. Put enough litter in to cover the whole of the base, to a thickness of two to three centimetres.

The right sort

Make sure that the litter you use is not too fine or dusty, or it may hurt your rats' eyes and get up their noses, making it hard to breathe. Don't use paper bedding or wood shavings that have been treated with aromatic oils – this is sometimes called 'deodorised bedding'. There can be chemicals called phenols in these types of bedding that will harm your rats' respiratory (breathing) system.

The litter you use will absorb the moisture from rats' urine and droppings.

Make a nest box

Rats need nest boxes to sleep in. You can buy these in pet shops, but you can also make your own, for example from an ice cream tub, a medium-sized plant pot or a small plastic bucket. Your rats will be happy to share a nest box, but you may want to put two or more in their cage.

Cosy bed

You will need to fill your rats' nest box with the right kind of bedding, which will soak up any moisture and make a snug bed. You can buy rat bedding material from pet shops, or use kitchen towel or toilet rolls from home. Don't use cotton wool for bedding, as your rats could choke on this if they swallowed it.

Most types of shredded paper will make good bedding for your nest box.

Bed wetters

Rats are clean animals, but they do have a habit of wetting their nest boxes. Check your rats' nest box every day and remove wet bedding if necessary.

Paper shredder

If you give your rats kitchen towel for bedding material, don't bother to tear it up first. Your rats will have lots of fun shredding it all by themselves, and this will save you time and effort!

Questions & Answers

* **Can I put cat litter in my rat cage?**
Yes, but be careful which type you use. Only recycled paper cat litter is suitable for rats.

* **Can I use newspaper as bedding?**
Yes, but only if it is printed with non-toxic ink. If the ink runs when it is wet, then it is vegetable-based and safe for your rats – but be aware that it could stain the fur of light-coloured rats.

* **Can I use straw or hay as bedding?**
Yes, and some people like to do this, but it is not very good at getting rid of smells and soaking up liquid. If you do buy hay or straw, get it from a pet shop and not a farm, or it might have ticks and fleas that could make your rats ill.

Rat toys

Rats are playful and inquisitive, so it is very important for them to have a variety of things to play with. Most pet shops sell a good range of rat toys, but you can also make your own toys or use things that you find around the house.

Good toys

Baby and young rats really enjoy playing with toys. Suitable toys include bits of plastic drainpipe, large glass jars, cardboard boxes and even old clothes. Hamster and gerbil toys are also good for small rats to play with. You must make sure the toys you give your rats are not too small, or they may swallow them.

Use your imagination to create an interesting home for your pets.

Playground

Your rats' cage can be made into an exciting adventure playground for your pets. Simply attach ropes, hammocks, ladders or branches to the sides of the cage. You could also place small flowerpots and plastic tunnels on the cage floor to make a maze.

Climbing high

If you have a tall cage, don't forget to make good use of all the space. You can make extra shelves by sliding wipe-clean boards between the bars of the cage. Your rats will use these to climb on. You may need to fix a safety net under the shelves, in case your rats fall off them. Check first that the net is strong enough to take your rats' weight.

Your rats will enjoy the challenge of an obstacle course in a rat-proofed room.

Play time

Older rats are not very interested in toys, but like to play games with their cage mates. They also love human contact, so you must play with them. Let them run up your sleeves and rest on your shoulders. Have some fun by laying out obstacle courses for your rats – you could use cardboard tubes, ladders, mirrors and balls.

Balancing act

Rats use their tails to keep their balance. A rat's tail can be as long as its body.

Wheel problem

It is not a good idea to put a wire exercise wheel in your rats' cage. They are too small for adult rats, and if a rat catches its tail between the bars, it will get a nasty injury. Plastic wheels are also dangerous for rats, because they may chew the plastic and reach the sharp metal spikes behind.

Questions & Answers

✳ **Can my rats have too many toys?**
Yes, be careful not to fill the cage with so many toys that your rats don't have any space left to run around in.

✳ **Will my rats chew their toys?**
Yes, rats chew almost everything! Give your rats a chew from a pet shop to help keep their teeth short.

✳ **If I put branches in my rats' cage, should I take the bark off?**
No, bark will help to keep your rats' nails short. However, you should make sure that any branches you put in the cage haven't been sprayed with pesticides. Pesticides can harm your rat.

21

Food and diet

Rats are omnivores, which means they eat all kinds of food. It is best to give your rats fresh, wholesome food to eat. Don't give too much of any one thing – your rats' diet should be varied and healthy, just like yours should be. Don't overfeed your rats or they will become fat.

Pet shop food

You can buy ready-mixed rat food from pet shops. Often, your rats will like one part of the mix more than the rest, and may try to leave the bits they don't like. Give your rats a small amount of the mix at a time, and only give them some more when the first lot is all eaten. You should also put a mineral lick in your rats' cage to give them nutrients that may be missing from their diet.

Fruit and vegetables are an essential part of a healthy diet for rats.

Fruit and vegetables

Your rats need fibre in their diet, so they must eat fresh fruit and vegetables. Avoid acidic fruits like oranges, but try other fruits, for example apples and bananas. Your rats will enjoy trying different vegetables, such as carrots and curly kale. Don't give them too much fruit or too many vegetables, or your rats may get tummy upsets. It's best to offer your rats fruit and vegetables every other day.

Treats

You can give your rats healthy, tasty treats to spice up their diet. They will enjoy many different foods, including low protein dog biscuits, cooked bones, cooked pulses (for example lentils), live yoghurt, unsweetened cereals, brown pasta, brown bread and brown rice. Don't offer your rats sweet or salty snacks, such as chocolate, cakes, ice cream or crisps. These snacks are bad for their health.

Fresh water

It is very important to give your rats fresh, cool water every day, preferably in a water bottle. Scrub the bottle with a bottlebrush once a week to keep it clean. Remember to replace it every few months with a new one.

Handing over

When you go on holiday, make sure the person who is going to look after your rats knows what to feed them, and when. You will probably need to write down some instructions. You should also leave details of someone to phone in an emergency.

Don't let your rats run out of drinking water, especially on hot days.

Questions & Answers

✱ **When should I feed my rats?**
It is often best to feed rats in the evening, as this is when they are at their most active.

✱ **How much food should I give my rats?**
It is a good idea to give food in small amounts, then more if necessary. If your rats are leaving a lot of food, you are probably overfeeding them.

✱ **How often should I give my rats a food treat?**
Save treats until after your rats have eaten up their main food. Don't give too much, just a taste, for example a few dog biscuit crumbs, or a small spoonful of live yoghurt.

Regular routine

Rats like to have a regular routine. Feed your rats at the same time every day. They will soon learn when to expect food, and will be waiting for you.

Keeping clean

You must remember to clean out your rats' cage regularly, or it will become an unpleasant and unhealthy place for them to live. The cage will begin to smell and your family will probably start to complain! Cleaning out your rats' cage isn't difficult, and it won't take you long to do.

Cleaning out your rats' cage should become part of your regular weekly routine. Always remember to wash your hands afterwards.

Clean cage

When you clean out your rats' cage, first take out the toys and throw away the litter and bedding. Wipe down the surfaces with a mild disinfectant, bought from a pet shop. Remember to wipe the toys and branches too. Then wash off the disinfectant with some water. When everything is dry, put fresh bedding back into the cage. Don't forget to wear plastic gloves when you clean out your rats' cage.

Daily check

You should also do a small clear-out every day. Remove any unwanted food and droppings scattered about the cage floor. Check that the bedding is clean and dry, scooping out any wet material and replacing it with fresh bedding. Wash the food bowl and remember to clean the water bottle if necessary.

Bath time

Rats spend a lot of time grooming themselves and each other. You shouldn't have to wash your rats' coats to keep them clean. However, if you want to enter your rats for a show, you may need to bathe them. Use lukewarm water and small animal shampoo when you do this.

Great groomers

Rats spend about one third of their waking life grooming themselves.

Tail trouble

Some rats don't clean their tails very well. You can remove stains on your rats' tails by brushing them with a soft toothbrush and some small animal shampoo. Wet the tail first, then carefully brush away from the body towards the tip. Be very gentle – rough brushing will hurt your rats.

Rats are naturally very clean animals.

Water fun

Every now and again, give your rats some water in a bowl. A dog water bowl is best, because it is too heavy for them to tip over. Your rats will like to use the water to wash in. You could encourage them to play in the water by putting in a few frozen peas. Your rats will get very wet!

Questions & Answers

* **How often should I clean my rats' cage?**
You should clean your rats' cage once or twice a week. Don't clean it out every day, or your rats will feel insecure – rats don't like it when their own smell is removed too often. Male rats will scent-mark more frequently if you 'overclean' their cage.

* **Where should I put my rats when I am cleaning out their cage?**
You could put them in a rat-proofed room, with someone to watch them. Alternatively, you can buy a rat carrier. These come in very handy for trips to the vet and are also a good place to put your rats when you're cleaning out their cage.

* **What is the best way to bath my rat?**
Fill two bowls with lukewarm water. Use one for washing your rat with small animal shampoo, and the other for rinsing your rat. Have a soft towel to hand to gently dry your rat after its bath.

Health check

You need to check your rats regularly to make sure that they are keeping fit and well. A healthy rat should be lively, alert and keen to eat its food. It should have a shiny and well-groomed coat and clean ears and tail. Its droppings shouldn't be too hard or too runny, and there should be no bumps or swellings on its body.

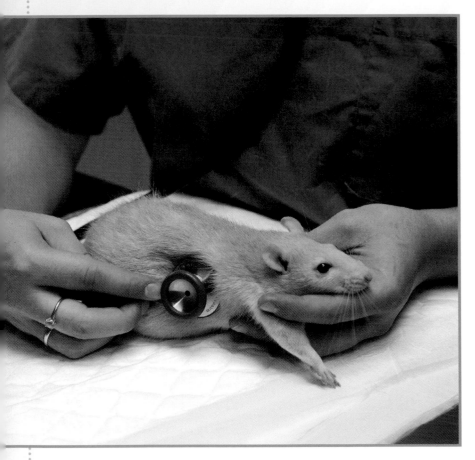

A good vet will tell you what to do if your rat gets ill.

Get a vet

Rats are small animals, which means if they get ill, they can go downhill very fast. Make sure you find a good local vet as soon as you get your rats. This way, you will know where to go quickly if one of your rats becomes unwell.

Warning signs

It is not a good sign if one of your rats is hunched up in its cage and looks too tired to move. Listen to your rat's breathing, and take note if it is wheezy. If your rat loses interest in you and its food, and its coat starts to look scruffy, you must take it to the vet.

Body language

Keep an eye on how your rat moves around in the cage. If it has a limp, it may be injured and in pain. If it holds its head on one side, it may have an ear problem. In both cases, you should go straight to the vet.

Long in the tooth

A rat's teeth never stop growing. Rats need to gnaw and chew things to keep their teeth short.

Tooth and nail

A rat with overgrown teeth won't be able to eat properly, and can even starve. If your rat's teeth don't meet properly, they will need regular trimming by a vet to stop them from growing too long. Check your rat's teeth often, and get them trimmed if they look overgrown. It is also important to have your rat's nails clipped regularly. Get a vet or an adult to do this for you, using small animal nail clippers.

You can check your rat's nails and teeth when you are playing with your pet.

Weight problem

Once your rats are adults, they should stay at about the same weight. If they suddenly lose or gain weight, they could be ill. Don't overfeed your rats – fat rats live shorter lives and are more likely to get sick. Healthy does should be lean and sleek, and bucks should be strong and muscular.

Questions & Answers

* **What should I do if my rat looks ill?**
First of all talk about it with an adult, then ask if they can take you and your pet to the vet. You may have to give your rat antibiotics to clear up an infection.

* **Will my rat get better?**
Rats can get ill quickly, but given the right treatment, they can also make good recoveries. But obviously, it depends exactly what is wrong with your rat, and only a vet will know that.

* **How do I know if my rat's teeth and nails are too long?**
If your rat's teeth are too long, they won't bite food properly and your rat will find it hard to eat. If your rat's nails are too long, they will scratch you when you pick up your pet.

Old age

Rats need company, exercise and a healthy diet to live a full and happy life. But sadly, however well and carefully you look after your rats, they will still grow old. As rats get older, they slow down, get weaker and become prone to illness. You need to give your old rats a quiet life, with lots of gentle care and affection.

If your rat gets heatstroke, cover it carefully with a damp towel.

Catching a cold

Just like you, rats are prone to catching colds, and they are more likely to do this in old age. Watch out for a runny nose, red eyes, wheezes and sneezes. If your rat gets a cold, keep it warm and give it lots of water to drink. Take it to the vet, as it probably won't get better on its own.

Watch the heat

It is always important to watch the temperature, especially for older rats. If your rat gets too hot, it could get heat stroke. You will need to wrap your rat in a damp towel to cool it down.

Keeping warm

If your old rat gets cold, it could also become ill. You can revive your rat by popping it under your jumper to warm it up with your body temperature.

Some older rats can't see very well, and are not as active as they used to be.

Head for heights

Old rats become less agile and their eyesight may deteriorate. Some rats may also lose their sense of balance. It is a good idea to remove any ladders, branches and climbing toys from their cage, so that they won't fall off and hurt themselves.

A rat's life

Most rats live for about two and a half years, but some can live for up to four years.

Saying goodbye

Many rats die naturally of old age. But if your rat is very sick, it may be kindest to talk to your vet about having it put to sleep. This is completely painless for your rat, and a peaceful, gentle way to say goodbye to your old friend.

Questions & Answers

✴ **Will my rat look old?**
When your rat is about two years old, it will start to look old. Its coat will get thinner and it will begin to move more stiffly.

✴ **Should I bury my pet when it dies?**
Some people find that it helps them to make a special burial place in the garden for their pet.

✴ **How can I remember my rat?**
Take lots of photos of your rat throughout its life. Make a scrapbook, and label the pictures. You will enjoy looking at the photos, and remembering the fun you had with your pet.

Glossary

alert
Lively, watchful and interested in everything.

antibiotics
Medicines used to treat infectious diseases.

bedding
Soft material used to provide a warm, comfortable bed.

breed
To have babies.

bucks
Male rats are called bucks.

diet
The food that animals usually eat. Rats should have a varied and healthy diet.

does
Female rats are called does.

fancy rats
Pet rats are called fancy rats. Unlike wild rats, fancy rats have special colours or patterns on their fur.

grooming
Grooming is cleaning an animal's coat. Rats spend lots of time grooming themselves and each other.

hormonal
This means controlled by hormones. Hormones are chemicals made in the bodies of plants and animals that affect their actions and responses.

kittens
Baby rats are called kittens.

litter
A litter is a group of baby rats born at the same time, with the same mother. Litter is also the material you use to line the bottom of your rats' cage.

mineral lick
A solid block for your rats to lick, containing nutrients that could be missing from their diet.

nest box
A snug place for your rats to rest and sleep, that is both warm and secure.

nursing female
A female rat that is feeding milk to her newborn babies.

omnivores
Animals that eat all kinds of food, both plants and meat.

predator
An animal that hunts other animals.

put to sleep
To give a sick animal an injection to help it die peacefully.

rodents
A group of small, gnawing animals that includes rats, mice, hamsters, gerbils, squirrels and beavers.

scent-marking
A male rat's habit of marking out territory with a few drops of his urine.

species
A group of one type of animal or plant.

territory
An area that belongs to a single individual.

vermin
Vermin are animals that cause problems for people, often by carrying diseases. Pet rats are not vermin, but wild rats are.

Further information

If you want to learn more about types of rats, buying rats, looking after rats, or if you would like to get involved in animal welfare, these are some helpful websites:

UNITED KINGDOM
National Fancy Rat Society
Good source of information about keeping fancy rats. The website has a calendar of rat shows throughout the UK.
Website: www.nfrs.org
Contact address:
NFRS, PO Box 24207, London, United Kingdom, SE9 5ZF

Another good UK pet rat website with helpful information:
www.fancy-rats.co.uk

Royal Society for the Prevention of Cruelty to Animals (RSPCA)
Campaigning charity for animals. Useful source of pet keeping information.
Website: www.rspca.org.uk
Contact address:
Enquiries service, RSPCA, Wilberforce Way, Southwater, Horsham, West Sussex, United Kingdom RH13 9RS.

AUSTRALIA
Australian Rat Fanciers Society
This society has branches all over Australia. Check the website for details.
Website: www.ausrfs.org.au
Contact address:
PO Box 15, Heidelberg West, Victoria, Australia 3018

Australian Mouse and Rat Information Service (AMRIS)
AMRIS aims to improve the way people treat rats and other pet rodents.
Contact address:
PO Box 4248, Ringwood, Victoria, Australia 3134

UNITED STATES OF AMERICA
Rat and Mouse Club of America (RMCA)
Good source of information about keeping fancy rats. The club hosts regular rat keeping events.
Website: www.rmca.org
Contact address:
RMCA, 6082 Modoc Road, Westminster, CA 92683, USA

American Fancy Rat and Mouse Association (AFRMA)
AFRMA promotes and encourages the breeding and exhibition of fancy rats and mice. It gives useful information on how to look after them.
Website: www.afrma.org
Contact address:
AFRMA, 9230 64TH St, Riverside, CA 92509 – 5924, USA

Note to parents and teachers: Every effort has been made by the Publishers to ensure that these websites are suitable for children, that they are of the highest educational value, and that they contain no inappropriate or offensive material. However, because of the nature of the Internet, it is impossible to guarantee that the contents of these sites will not be altered. We strongly advise that Internet access is supervised by a responsible adult.

Index